MARRIED BLITZ!

LANG SYNE   PUBLISHERS LTD.

Published by Lang Syne Publishers Ltd.,
45 Finnieston Street, Glasgow G3 8JU.
Tel: 0141-204 3104
Printed by Dave Barr Print,
45 Finnieston Street, Glasgow G3 8JU.
Tel: 0141-221 2598

First published 1988. Reprinted 1995.

ISBN No. 185217 120 0

INTRODUCTION

Marriage is a great institution — but as the man once said, who wants to spend their life in an institution?

An important weapon in the marriage survival stakes though, is having a sense of humour.

Your partner, your kids and your mother-in-law will at times drive you demented.

But do not despair. This hilarious book has been lovingly created to help you appreciate the funny side of it all.

"Never mind, dear. Just think of it as making the national average of 2.5 times this week."

Marriage Lines!

If it wasn't for marriage folk could go through life thinking they were totally faultless.

✳   ✳   ✳   ✳   ✳   ✳

There's a lot in the wise old saying: Don't marry the one you love, marry the one who loves you.

✳   ✳   ✳   ✳   ✳   ✳

MacDougall screamed at his wife that she was a lousy cook, a lousy housekeeper, a lousy lover, then he stormed out of the house.

That night MacDougall got home to find her in the arms of a stranger.

"What on earth are you doing?" he screamed.

"Getting a second opinion" she replied acidly.

✳   ✳   ✳   ✳   ✳   ✳

"Darling, isn't that sign supposed to go on the door?"

"You've missed a bit in the corner."

"Somehow, Edna, you always manage to take the romance out of it!"

DUNSTRIPPIN'

"Couldn't you find some other way of saying you're a retired decorator?"

DIARY

JUST MARRIED

"How do you spell 'squib'?"

"FETCH HIM!"

"Face facts, Bert — they're onto you!"

"Harold, look — my honeymoon dress!"

MISSING PERSONS

"But Madam — we found your husband 2 weeks ago!"

"You'll have to excuse my husband's speech, officer — he's had a little too much to drink!"

Signing on ....

A marriage licence is an important document. Without one you can't get a divorce.

* * * *

Mr Mack and Mrs Mack had a 50-50 property settlement.
She got the house and he got the mortgage.

* * * *

Love is ....

Asking yourself bluntly: If it ends in divorce would I mind being financially destroyed by this person?

* * * *

Alan ran off from his wife. Now their lawyers are arguing over the legal position. She wants him sued for desertion. All he'll admit to is leaving the scene of an accident.

MUCH ADO ABOUT NOTHING

MORRIS

"I EVEN HAVE TO WASH AND
IRON MY OWN APRON!"

"Your wife's visiting her
sister. I'm the baby sitter."

10

"No - there's nothing wrong with the physical side to our marriage — I thump him most nights!"

11

Mothers-in-Law!

Jack's mother-in-law was so ugly that her first child refused to breastfeed from her until she covdred up her face.
The neighbourhood peeping tom once complained to the police because she kept her curtains open at night.

•••••••••

My mother-in-law looks like a million dollars — all green and wrinkled.

•••••••••

At the computer dating agency MacLeod's mother-in-law was told her ideal mate had been extinct for four million years.

•••••••••

I'm not saying my mother-in-law is a sour woman but she uses lashings of lemon juice for her complexion.

Agony is ....

Behind every successful man is ....
.... a mother-in-law saying what a failure he is.

•••••••••

I can't understand men who don't know how to address their mothers-in-law. I've always found 'Sir' works a treat.

•••••••••

Archie's mother-in-law has got a new job. She's the decoy for a whaling fleet.

•••••••••

My mother-in-law has to speak through her nose. Her mouth is worn out.

•••••••••

My mother-in-law puts a pint of milk on the mantelpiece and stares at it. Yes, she's very fond of yoghurt.

•••••••••

Being a bigamist and having two mothers-in-law.

"You turned over two pages of that
sex manual at once dear."

13

"Maybe they've gone back to your place, Martha!"

"Mother! I can handle this date myself!"

14

"He tried to contradict me, once."

"I still think it's a bit showy for a blind date, Esther."

"Oh, come on now, you know you always turn back at Dover ..."

THE IGLOO

'I don't give you frozen food that often!"

"Typical, just our luck!"

"Excuse me. Do you believe in love at first FRIGHT?"

"Before we start with the birds and bees, let's have a look at your stocks and shares!"

18

Sailor's Riddle.

The sailor told the doctor he couldn't understand why his wife was pregnant as he'd been at sea for more than twelve months.

"Well, I'm afraid it's what I call a grudge pregnancy" explained the doc.

"Someone had it in for you."

* * * * * *

Heart to Heart

The heart patient was given the latest pills from America for his condition. His consultant described them as a miracle cure which would have him better in a short period.

The consultant told him to take a tablet on Monday, Wednesday and Friday, and to skip the other days.

Three weeks later the man dropped dead.

"I just can't understand it" said the consultant to the widow. "These tablets are being hailed as wonders."

"Oh, it wasnt the tablets that did it, doctor," said the widow. "It was all that skipping that knackered him."

* * * * * *

Chatting it up

John spotted a lovely young woman in the street and decided to try and chat her up.

"Hello beautiful, I'm sure we've met before" he said.

"I doubt it," said the girl with an icy stare.

"Oh sorry," said John, now trying to be sarcastic. "I thought you were my mother."

"No, that's impossible," she replied. "I'm married."

* * * * * *

Love is ....

Mary called off her wedding to Jack blaming her shock decision on religious differences. He was poor and she worshipped money.

* * * * * *

"Of course I'm marrying you for love.
You're rich, and I love rich men!"

20

"GEORGE!"

"Last thing I remember was my wife saying,
'Be an angel and let me drive'!"

"I've lost a brown cocker spaniel. My husband took him
for a walk and they haven't come back."

x

22

"I really must go now. Joe wants me to darn his socks."

Hamish knows best!

When the doctor had completed his annual check-up Hamish MacHearty confided that he was to marry the widow MacDonald on his 70th birthday .... which was just five days away.

"My, that's wonderful news," said the doctor.

"And you couldn't be in better shape judging from to-day's examination. But a wee word of caution, Hamish. Mrs MacDonald has got acute angina so ...."

But before he could finish Hamish chipped in: "Don't I know it, doctor. Don't I know it!"

* * * * * *

All tied up!

A vasectomy means never having to say you're sorry.

* * * * * *

Those Kids!

"Daddy's upstairs teaching Auntie Linda to trampoline, Mummy."

*"Mummy, do you think the milkman
would like to buy a polaroid?"*

"And remember, Daddy wil spank you if you tell him about this naughty dream you're having."

"Sharon won't be long — she's just finishing
her pickles and ice-cream."

"He's getting warm isn't he, Dad?"

29

"But how can it be morning here
and evening where you are?"

"Thanks for the lecture on sex, Dad, but when I asked
where I came from I couldn't remember if it was
Bathgate or Dalkeith!"

31

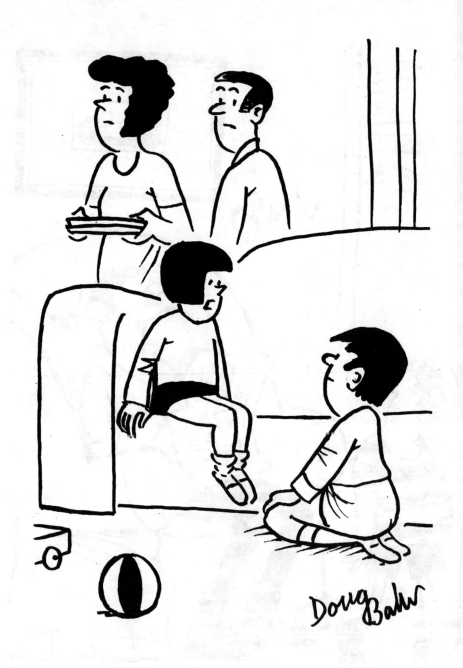

*"We won't play mothers and fathers —
I can't nag and you're not mean with money!"*

"I put all your five-pound notes in the big money box on the street corner, Daddy."

"How do we know it's not infested with sharks?"

"Haven't you heard of OPEN prisons?"

"Guess how many wires there are in your hi-fi system, Dad."

33

"I wish you wouldn't squeeze me when I'm soapy!"

"There's something wrong here — when I'm wide awake I have to go to bed, and when I'm asleep I have to get up!"

35

"Just one more question, Dad — why do I ask so many stupid questions?"

"I don't care if your Dad **is** stronger than my Dad — my Mum's older than yours!"

"When your father was at school, history was called current events."

"Now Jeremy's old enough for us to stand him, he can't stand US!"

"Sure, my wages go into five figures — wife and four sons!"

"If it's not bye bye with our Susan, it's buy buy!"

"We'll call this one Sue and the other Di for divorce!"

"I do envy you your freedom."

"Mum, Dad, may I inflict Ted on you?"

"But if the films were in black and white, Dad, why were they called blue films?"

"Get me a glass of water while you're up, will you, Dad?"

"Why is it you never suggest we get an early night any more, dear?"

39

"Your mother and I have been meaning to tell you
something for some time — you're adopted."

More about that woman!

Murphy's mother-in-law has an enormous rear end. When she walks down the street it looks like two little lads fighting under a blanket.

••••••••••••••••••••

What did the cannibal enjoy most about his wedding? Toasting the mother-in-law!

••••••••••••••••••••

Murphy's mother-in-law hung her knickers out on the line to dry. And a family of tinkers came along and set up camp under them.

••••••••••••••••••••

I'm going to be buried far out at sea when I die — because my mother-in-law has threatened to dance on my grave.

••••••••••••••••••••

MacKenzie's mother-in-law talked so much on holiday her tongue got sunburned.

••••••••••••••••••••

Murphy's not saying his mother-in-law is fat but once he was dancing with her for half an hour before realising that she was still sitting down.

••••••••••••••••••••

We all have a soft spot for our mothers-in-law. It's called a swamp.

••••••••••••••••••••

"I promise I'll never be a burden to you, darling."

"Marry in haste, yes. But where's all this leisure we're supposed to repent at?"

"It's the last time we come out and eat muck like this — we'll eat it at home in future."

"Damn blister on my foot, dear."

Naughty Angus!

Angus was down in London for a few days and on the second evening used the services of a lady of leisure in Soho.

When their business was completed he gave her £100.

"No one has ever given me that amount before — so much for the image of mean Scots. Which part are you from?"

"Aberdeen" relplied Angus.

"Really," said the lady. "My father's an Aberdonian."

"I know," said Angus. "When he knew I would be in London he asked me to give you £100."

* * * * * *

"I've really enjoyed today. I must do this more often."

Cafe Sign!

Don't divorce your wife because she can't cook.
Eat here — keep her as a pet.

* * * * * *

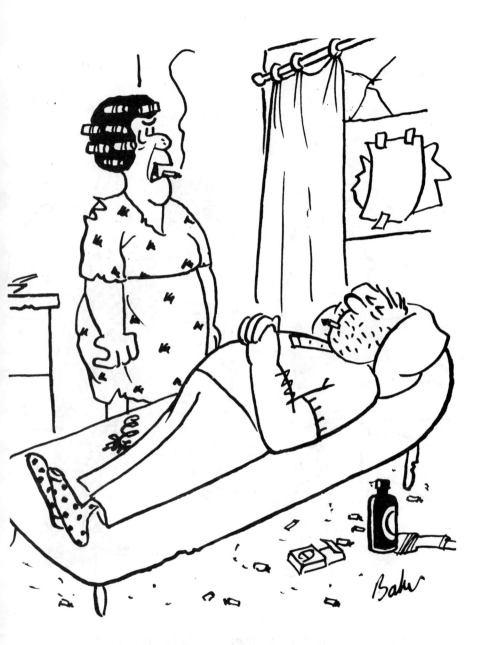

"I was a fool to marry you.
I should've married Robert Redford."

"You must drink a lot. Mum told Dad to keep away from you because of the smell of beer."

"She's either called you catty, ratty, or fatty, dear!"

"You don't trust me throwing him into the air and having some fun, do you?"

"Either my missus has played a practical joke on me or he's cleverer than I thought!"

"Who's only six weeks old and has more hair than Daddy?"

47

"I wish you'd call here before you deliver to Mrs King."

*"Now why can't you buy a dress
shaped like that, Mildred?"*

49

Paying up ....

My sister-in-law reckons she's the boss of the house cos my brother hands her his pay packet unopened every month.
She doesn't know he gets paid every fortnight.

* * * * * *

Glorious mud!

Paddy told his mates over the Guinness that the new mud pack definitely improved his wife's appearance, Sadly, it fell off after a few days.

* * * * * *

Silent sense ....

My neighbour hasn't spoken to his wife for eight years.
He says he doesn't like to interrupt.

* * * * * *

"What's happening to us, Doris?
We seem to be drifting apart."

"CAUGHT YOU!"

"That one is definitely you — outdated and hideous!"

Fireproof!

MacLeod died and went to hell but after a few weeks was making such a nuisance of himself that the Devil threatened to throw him out.

"You're going around as if you owned the place," said Auld Nick.

"And why shouldn't I — my mother-in-law gave it to me when I was alive," said MacLeod.

● ● ● ● ● ● ● ● ● ●

Plastic-proof!

My wife has had so many face-lifts that the plastic surgeons say they'll have to lower her body for any future ops.

* * * *

Did you hear about the marriage of the two light house keepers? It's on the rocks.

* * * *

"And one day, darling, the patter of tiny comedians."

"Their marriage is so precarious the Marriage Guidance counsellor lives in with them."

"Mum! She broke our engagement and returned what I gave her!"

She's back again!

Murphy told his mother-in-law that if she lived in India she'd be sacred. Think about it ....

• •

I didn't say that my mother-in-law was a bad cook. All I said was that the mice take in their own sandwiches. And the Indians dip their arrows in her stew.

• • • • • • • • • • • • • • • • • • • •

When my mother-in-law goes to the zoo they give her a special pass to get out again.

• • • • • • • • • • • • • • • • • • • •

We'd a lot of fun on holiday last year burying mother-in-law in the sand. We may go back again this year and dig her up.

• • • • • • • • • • • • • • • • • • • •

I was perfectly happy for 23 years. So was my mother-in-law. Then we met.

• • • • • • • • • • • • • • • • • • • •

Asked to define a monologue a downtrodden dad told his son: "A monologue is a conversation between a man and his mother-in-law."

• • • • • • • • • • • • • • • • • • • •

My mother-in-law caused a bit of a problem in the Chamber of Horrors at Edinburgh Wax Museum. They were stock-taking at the time.

• • • • • • • • • • • • • • • • • • • •

"I got stuck in a telephone box but I talked my way out of it!"

"I was drunk all right. I felt sophisticated but couldn't pronounce it!"

"What I liked best about my mother's cooking was it didn't cost me anything!"

"It's his knee. I found his secretary on it!"

"I wish I'd never told you I wanted a stable life when we got married."

Sex-cess?

The doctor was firing questions at the businessman in the course of the annual check-up.

"Sex?" asked the doctor.

"Infrequently" said the businessman.

"Is that one word or two?" asked the doc, delicately.

* * * * * *

The next lesson ....

Constable to drunk: "Where are you going at this time of night in that condition?"

Drunk: "To a lecture."

Constable: "A lecture. Who's giving it?"

Drunk: "The wife."

* * * * * *

Fireproof!

I'm not saying Freddie is nasty but he keeps a picture of his mother-in-law above the fireplace to keep the kids away from the fire.

* * * * * *

HOLY ....

A young Glasgow man, brought up in the Protestant faith, turned Catholic and went to confession for the first time. He confessed to adultery.
"How many times, son?" asked the priest.
"Crivvens", replied the man, "I didn't come here to boast!"

* * * *

....SMOKE!

Jimmy arrived home unexpectedly to find his wife in bed with a big cigar smouldering in the ashtray on the bedside cabinet.
"Where did that come from?" he boomed.
"Havana" muttered a voice from inside the wardrobe.

* * * *

Seriously?

Scotland's high divorce rate makes us the land of the free.
But the soaring marriage rate must, by the same token, make us the land of the brave.

* * * *

"It's okay if you left the iron on at home. I left the tap running and that should put any fire out!"

"I was absolutely delighted with the wedding — I can hardly wait till the next one!"

59

"For Pete's sake close your mouth, Ethel."

"Your husband says he fails to see how his marriage
has led to divorce, and he'll join us as soon
as the pubs close."

"Did they not have a
mirror in the shop?"

"I don't like school. I can't
read or write and they
won't let me talk!"

"I'd like to marry a rich girl
who is too proud to let her
husband work!"

"Fred's the dearest, most
loving husband in the
world. Too bad I married
Paul!"

When is a wife's knowledge a husband's faith?
Well, a wife knows that the children are hers but the husband has just got to believe it.

*   *   *   *   *   *

The police patrol car flagged down Walter MacTavish on the Aberdeen — Dundee road to tell him that his wife had fallen out some 20 miles further back down the highway.
"Thank goodness for that" said MacTavish. "Ah thocht Ah'd gone deaf."

*   *   *   *   *   *

Dougie: "The doctor's told me that I must give up half of my sex life."
Seamus: "Which half? Talking about it .... or thinking about it?"

*   *   *   *   *   *

'You did say you haven't been married before, didn't you?"

The dad ....

Who'd be the father of the bride. He spends a small fortune on the arrangements culminating in a slap-up reception but the local paper always says how he gave the bride away!

Jim's missus said she fancied something for her neck for Christmas. So he bought her a bar of soap.

Murder most foul!

Defendant in court: "When I murdered my mother-in-law it was not pre-meditated. If it it was I'd have done it years ago."

* * * * * *

"I've just been telling these nice gentlemen how well we've been doing since you got that job at the bank, dear."

"I saw you staring at her legs!"

"Your new hairstyle suits you, dear — it's horrible!"

"There's been quite a change since Frank took up weight training — his face is redder!"

"For heavens sake stop sulking."

"And then he said, you couldn't even fight his Mum."

"Well, it started when he insisted on coming on the honeymoon with Mother and me."

"How do you wipe an annoying smile off your boyfriend's face? — Marry him."

*"I've had bad luck with both husbands.
The first divorced me and the second won't!"*

Sex is ....

The definition of sex .... the most fun you can have without laughing.

Old age is ....

Making dates your body can't keep.

* * * * * *

Wisdom is ....

My good friend McTavish believes in long engagements.
He says they make marriages shorter.

* * * * * *

"They're crows feet all right — and it looks
as if it's walked all over your face!"

"Somebody told him that if we could all trace our family trees back far enough, we'd find that we're related to royalty."

"Yes, it does look nice doesn't it — here's the recipe, but don't forget to leave out the poison!"

"What do you mean, hair-drier? This is my new hat."

"Let me be the first to congratulate you."

"We might as well not be here enjoying ourselves if you're going to gnash your teeth and disturb the fish."

"You didn't seem to enjoy yourself at the party, dear."

"Ever thought of giving your husband a nice big kiss now and then?"

"The joint's cooked, dear. Would you like to come and incise it?"

"Some wives have a burning desire to cook — mine has a cooking desire to burn."

"For 'passion breath'? That's me."

"Pull your stomach in, dear, I'm coming through."

"I would have preferred a rubber plant, Arnold."

"Always get married in the morning, son. In that way if it doesn't work out you haven't wasted the whole day!"

"Harold, have you seen my specs anywhere?"

"Please, darling, please find a boy and get married."

"Gone next door for a cup of sugar. Don't wait up for me. Ethel."

"You see, I told you it wouldn't last — they had to go and get married."

DUNFREEZIN

*"Personally, I've no sympathy for a bloke who wins
an argument with his missus and brags about it!"*

"Harold's been laid up in bed about a week now."

*"I don't mind you marrying
my daughter, son, if you're
sure she can support you."*

Happy daze!

Yes, I can thank my wife for five years of happy
marriage .... it's our twentieth anniversay tomorrow.

Doggy sense!

I'm not saying my wife's a bad cook but when some of
her dishes accidentally spill on the floor the dog
makes a bolt for the door.

*   *   *   *   *   *

"I wish you'd stop calling this an entanglement ring."

And finally ....

Marriage is a three-ring circus — the engagement ring, the wedding ring, and the suffering.

*   *   *   *   *   *